PHYSICAL SCIENCE

Turn on the
Light

How Electricity Works
Inside and Outside the Home

Ella Newell

Rourke
Publishing LLC
Vero Beach, Florida 32964

www.rourkepublishing.com

PHOTO CREDITS: p. 36: Natalia Bratslavsky/istockphoto.com; p. 31: Greg Brzezinski/ istockphoto.com; p. 17: Corbis; pp. 5, 37: Chris Fairclough/CFWImages.com; p. 12: Randy Faris/Corbis; p. 11: Stefan Hermans/istockphoto.com; p. 42: Honda; pp. 20, 22, 30: istockphoto.com; p. 9: Dr. Dennis Kunkel/Getty Images; p. 6: Lester Lefkowitz/Getty Images; p. 33: Mark Lewis/Getty Images; p. 16: Thomas Mounsey/istockphoto.com; p. 7: NASA; p. 4: Charlotte Nation/Getty Images; p. 18: Nuclear Energy Institute; p. 14, 43: Ed Parker/EASI-Images/ CFWImages.com; p. 26: Dave Peck/ istockphoto.com; p. 15: Photodisc; p. 41: PPM Energy; p. 32: Pali Rao/ istockphoto.com; p. 38: Harald Richter/NOAA Photo Library; OAR/ERL/National Severe Storms Laboratory (NSSL); p. 23: Steven Robertson/ istockphoto.com; p. 13: Krzysztf Rafal Siekielski/istockphoto.com; p. 34: Daniel St. Pierre/ istockphoto.com; p. 40: Rio Tinto plc/Newscast; p. 29: Edward Todd/ istockphoto.com; p. 39: Toyota; p. 35: Kirill Zdorov/istockphoto.com.

Cover picture shows light from a compact fluorescent lightbulb.
[Baldur Tryggvason/istockphoto.com]

Produced for Rourke Publishing by Discovery Books
Editors: Geoff Barker, Amy Bauman, Rebecca Hunter
Designer: Ian Winton
Cover designer: Keith Williams
Illustrator: Stefan Chabluk
Photo researcher: Rachel Tisdale

Library of Congress Cataloging-in-Publication Data

Newell, Ella.
  Turn on the light : how electricity works / Ella Newell.
     p. cm. -- (Let's explore science)
  Includes index.
  ISBN 978-1-60044-608-5
  1. Electricity--Juvenile literature. I. Title.
  QC527.2.N49 2008
  621.3--dc22
                                    2007020162

Printed in the USA

CONTENTS

chapter one

Power Plant to Bulb

You flip a switch, and a lightbulb glows. Your computer lights up when you turn it on. Do you know why? What keeps refrigerators cool? What heats water? The answer is electricity. This book tells the story of electricity's amazing journey from a huge power plant to the lights in your house.

Electricity is an invisible form of **energy**. At the flick of a switch, you can stop or start the flow of electricity. It looks like magic. But it's not! Look around your room. How many things need electricity to make them work? Remember to count objects that use batteries.

◀ *The batteries inside this computer are small stores of electricity.*

ZAP!

Your body depends on electricity, too. Did you count it among the things that use it? You have electricity in your body! An electrical charge keeps your heart beating.

▲*Electricity keeps cities and towns around the world working day and night.*

It's All About Energy!

Hospitals, schools, businesses, and sports centers all need electricity. They would come to a stop without it. Where does this energy come from? Most of the electricity we use comes from a power plant. Huge amounts of electricity are made here. Wires and cables carry it to our homes and businesses.

▼*X-rays, scanning machines, and other hospital equipment need a constant supply of electrical energy.*

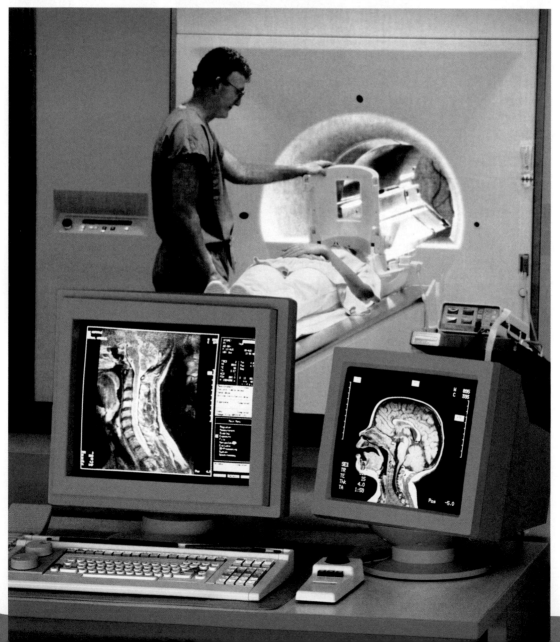

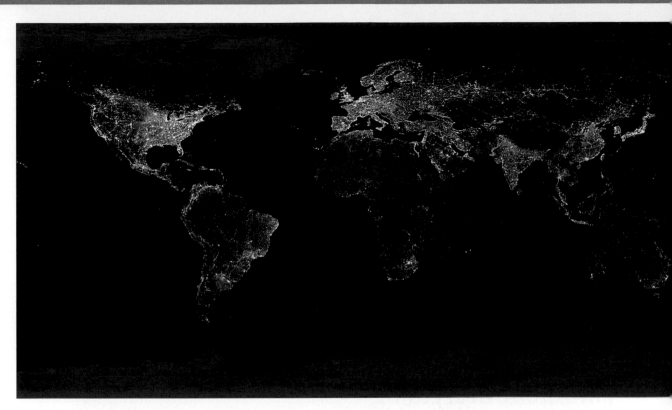

▲*In the dark, the Earth's surface glows brightly in areas where many lights are in use.*

Energy

Energy makes things work. There are many types of energy. Your body uses energy to run. A fire uses heat energy to cook food. Electricity is an energy that can be turned into other types of energy. It is used to make heat and light. This is what makes it so useful.

SAFETY!

Electricity can be dangerous. Maybe you know not to touch plugs or wires with wet hands. This is because electricity flows easily through water. Your body is mostly water. If you touch an electric current, you will get a shock. The electricity will flow through the water in your body.

chapter two

All About Electricity

So electricity makes the light glow when you flip on the switch. To understand why, we need to look at the tiniest bits of matter that make up our world.

All About Everything

Everything around us is made of **matter**. Matter is made up of tiny **atoms**. Imagine you tear a piece of aluminum foil in half. It still looks like foil. Now imagine you tear it up into thousands of pieces that can only be seen through a microscope. These pieces are called atoms.

▶ *The main parts of an atom.*

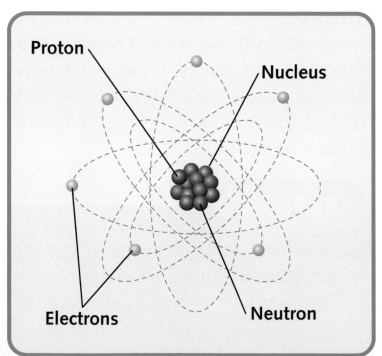

Proton

Nucleus

Electrons

Neutron

ATOMS

Atoms are so small you can only see them through a microscope. There are a million of them on one pin head!

All About Atoms

Each atom has a center called a nucleus. The nucleus is made up of tiny parts, or particles. These are called **protons** and **neutrons**. Circling the nucleus are more particles. These are **electrons**. Each electron has an electrical charge. They jump from atom to atom to create an electrical current. It takes the movement of about six billion electrons every second to light a lightbulb!

Current Electricity

Electrons move, or hop, from atom to atom. This creates a flow of electrical charge. This flow is called a current.

Sometimes an electrical charge can build up in one place. This is called **static electricity**. When electrical charge flows from one place to another, it is called current electricity. Current electricity is made in power plants and flows along wires and cables. This gives power to electrical products or appliances around your home.

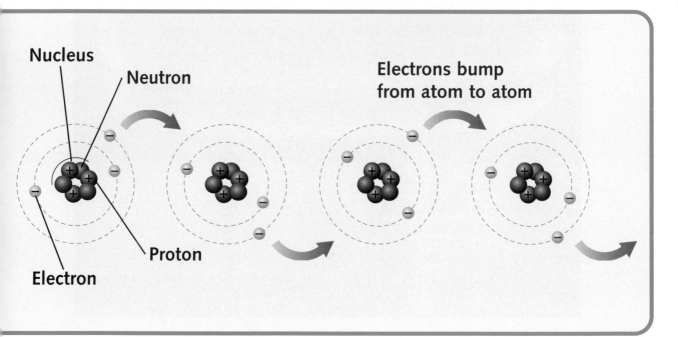

Nucleus

Neutron

Electrons bump from atom to atom

Proton

Electron

▲ *The flow of electrons jumping from atom to atom creates an electric current.*

Bump!

Light, heat, or a chemical reaction can make electrons move from one atom to another. As the electrons bump from atom to atom they create an electrical flow. The **electrical current** runs in a path like a circular running track, called a **circuit**.

▲*Imagine a row of dominoes. One falls and knocks the others down, one by one. Electrons bump from atom to atom in a similar way.*

+ and -

A proton has a positive charge. This is shown as the symbol +. An electron has a negative charge. This is shown as the symbol -. An unequal number of positive or negative charges produces an electrical charge.

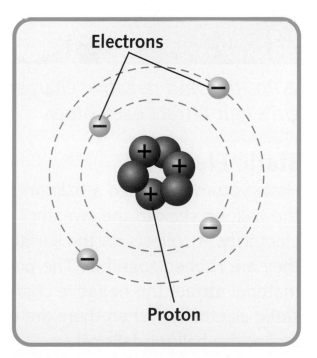

▶*When there are more negatively charged electrons than positively charged protons, it creates an electrical charge.*

▲*Positive and negative charges on the balloon and the girl's hair attract each other.*

Static Electricity

Have you ever rubbed a balloon against a sweater? Did the balloon stick to the sweater? This is caused by static electricity. It collects on the surfaces of some materials when they are rubbed together. The positive charges on one material attract the negative charges on the other. This makes static electricity. When there are equal numbers of charges again, the balloon falls off.

Opposites Attract

Two objects with lots of positively charged particles (protons) come together. You will see the particles try to push each other away. Objects with opposite charges (protons and electrons) attract each other. This is because the different charges try to balance each other out. If you comb your hair on a dry day with a plastic comb, the comb attracts electrons. That leaves your hair with too many protons. Each strand of hair will try to move away from the others!

How It Works

Walk across the carpet. Your shoes will gather up negative electrons. These whizz around your body looking for positive protons. Then you touch a metal door knob. The electrons are pulled toward the protons in the metal. As they jump across to the metal, it produces a tiny electric shock.

PHOTOCOPIER

Static electricity is used in photocopiers. Inside the machine, positively charged particles attract particles of black powder. The black powder is used to copy the image.

Lightning

It is a stormy day. The flash of lightning you see is a huge spark of electricity. Lightning is created by the attraction between opposite charges. This is the same force that creates static electricity. As electrons whirl inside a cloud or toward the ground, they heat the air around them. This creates the glow we see as lightning. What you are seeing is the path of electricity.

▲ *A flash of lightning contains enough energy to light a 100-watt bulb for three months!*

▲Lightning is attracted to the conductors (on the tallest building in the center of this photograph). The lightning then avoids striking nearby buildings and people in the area.

Discovery

Benjamin Franklin (1706–1790) was an American inventor. He discovered that lightning was a giant electrical spark. During a storm, he flew a kite with a metal key at the end of the string. Lightning flew down the string and created a spark on the key. Franklin then invented lightning rods. These are metal strips built on buildings. They carry lightning safely to the ground.

ENERGY IN A FLASH

Benjamin Franklin's experiment with the kite was dangerous. You should never try this. Lightning always looks for the quickest way to Earth. It will flow through any material through which electricity can flow. That includes human bodies.

15

All About Electricity and Magnetism

Magnetism is an invisible force. Some materials give it off. Magnetic force sometimes is used along with electricity. It is used to make electric motors. These provide the power for many of the machines and tools we use.

Magnetism

A magnet draws materials containing iron and nickel to it. Each magnet has a north pole and a south pole. Opposite poles attract each other.

◄*These iron filings are pulled toward the magnet.*

Electromagnets

An electrical current passes along a wire. It creates a magnetic field. Wrap the wire around an iron bar. Now, as the current passes through the wire, the magnetic field grows stronger. This is called an electromagnet. It works a lot like other magnets. But there is one big difference. You can stop the current in an electromagnet. Then the magnetic field turns off, too.

Electric Motors

An **electric motor** uses an electromagnet. It uses the magnetism to turn electrical energy into mechanical power. This is the power that makes things move. In the motor, a magnet is placed near an electromagnet. The two magnets react. A push and pull movement is created. This makes a turning movement to work a motor.

▲*Some trains float above a magnetic field. Electromagnets start and stop the train.*

chapter three

Making Electricity

Electricity is made by turning other forms of energy into electrical energy. This is what **power plants** do. There, fuels such as coal and oil are burned. This powers machines called **generators**. These machines produce electricity.

►*Nuclear power plants produce large amounts of energy. They use only small amounts of fuel.*

ALL DAY, EVERY DAY

Power plants cannot store the electricity they make. They make it twenty four hours a day, every day of the year. If they did not, there would not be enough electricity.

Steam to Electricity

Many power plants use coal. Burning the coal heats water and turns it into steam. The force of the steam turns large fan blades. These are connected to a pole that then turns a generator. Magnets spin around inside the generator. This makes electrons jump across coils of copper wire to produce a current of electricity.

Different fuels can be used to produce electricity. No matter which fuel is used, the electricity made is the same.

► *Which fuels were used most to make electricity in the United States in 2005?*

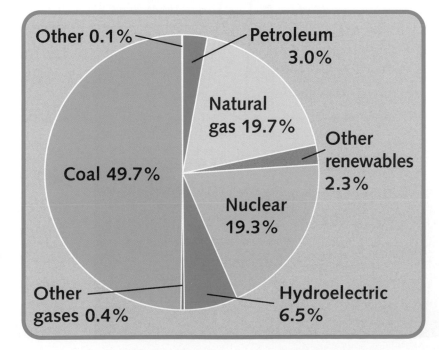

Other 0.1%
Petroleum 3.0%
Natural gas 19.7%
Other renewables 2.3%
Coal 49.7%
Nuclear 19.3%
Other gases 0.4%
Hydroelectric 6.5%

Sending Elecricity

Electricity is made and then sent to where it is needed. It flows out from the plant along wires and cables. These wires and cables carry the power to houses and businesses.

The Grid

The cables and wires that carry electricity crisscross the country. Together, they are known as the **grid**. They run underground, above ground, and even under the oceans. Wires that run above ground are carried between tall poles. In some places, the poles are replaced by tall towers.

◄*Tall towers called pylons support the electrical cables. Electricity can be sent around the country.*

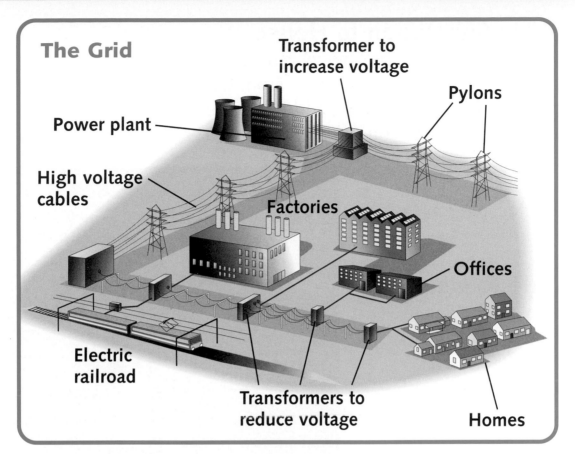

The Grid

Transformer to increase voltage

Pylons

Power plant

High voltage cables

Factories

Offices

Electric railroad

Transformers to reduce voltage

Homes

▲*Power plants produce electricity. Electricity travels along cables to supply factories, businesses, and homes.*

Voltage

The push of the electricity that leaves the power plant is very powerful. It is known as high **voltage**. This is too strong to use safely in houses and schools. So the electricity stops at a substation. Here, the voltage is reduced in a machine. It is called a **transformer**. The electricity then rolls on to villages, towns, and cities. It is safe to use.

FAST MOVER

Electricity moves at the speed of light. Light moves at more than 186,000 miles (300,000 kilometers) per second!

From Substation to House

At the substation, the voltage is reduced. Then the electricity continues on its way. From here, the electricity flows to factories, schools, and businesses. Before the electricity reaches your house, it passes to a meter. The meter will keep track of how much electricity people in your house use.

Safe to Use

Look outside your house or apartment. You may see an electrical pole with a small box on the side. This is a small transformer. It lowers the voltage even more before it is used in your house.

▶*Electricity produced in a power plant travels miles along cables and wires like these.*

ELECTRICITY AND WEATHER

Strong storms and icy weather can harm electricity poles. This can stop the flow of electricity. But in some places, cables are run underground. This protects them from the weather. It helps avoid power loss.

Ready and Waiting

A cable links your house to the grid that carries electricity from the power plant. Wires run through walls to outlets. Electricity is always waiting in the wires. With a flip of the switch, the circuit is closed. Electricity flows. To complete the circuit, other wires carry the electrical current back to the power plant.

chapter four

All in a Circuit

Flip a switch. You can start or stop the flow of electricity. The electricity used in homes flows along a wire in a circuit. A circuit is like a circle. The switch you press, turn, or flip, opens or closes the circuit. If there is a gap in the circuit, electrons cannot jump from atom to atom. There is no power. When there is no gap, the electrons can jump. Then the electricity flows to the object connected to the circuit.

What Makes a Circuit?

An electrical circuit needs:
- a source of electrical power (this could be a power plant or a battery)
- a material along which the electricity can flow (this may be a copper wire)
- something to power (this could be a bulb)

The circuit is connected in a loop. Then, the source of power pushes electrons around the wire. It lights the bulb and continues in the circuit until it is broken.

A simple circuit lights one bulb. More difficult circuits might have several switches and loops. This would allow different groups of lights to be turned on or off at the same time.

Simple Circuit

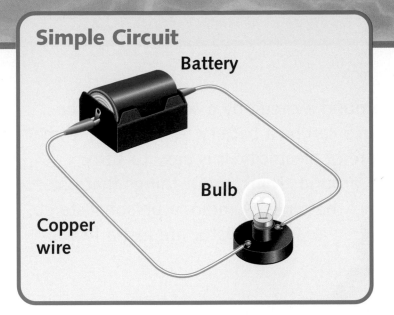

Battery

Bulb

Copper
wire

◀ *This simple circuit in one loop lights one bulb.*

Series Circuit

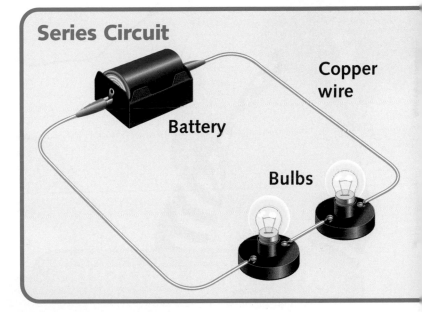

Copper
wire

Battery

Bulbs

▶ *A series circuit has only one path of electricity. Il provides power for more than one electrical load.*

Parallel Circuit

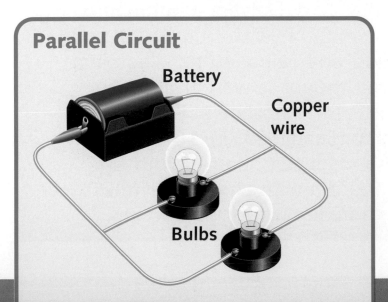

Battery

Copper
wire

Bulbs

◀ *In a parallel circuit, electricity can pass along different paths to power different loads.*

Battery Power

Electricity is pushed around a circuit by a source of power. This source can be a battery. A battery is a small store of electricity. It is easy to carry around. Think about things that use batteries. A radio, a personal stereo, and a calculator are just a few.

◄*Some modern batteries are very small. Some are even as small as a pencil tip!*

INVENTING BATTERIES

In 1780, scientist Luigi Galvani examined a dead frog. He touched it with two metal rods. The frog twitched and released an electrical current. Galvani thought it was caused by electricity in the frog. Another scientist, Alessandro Volta, disagreed. In 1800, he showed that the electricity came from the contact of the metals with the frog's moisture. Volta went on to design the first battery.

How a Battery Works

A battery has chemicals inside it. The battery is linked to a circuit. Then the chemicals inside the battery react together. This pushes a flow of electrons around the circuit.

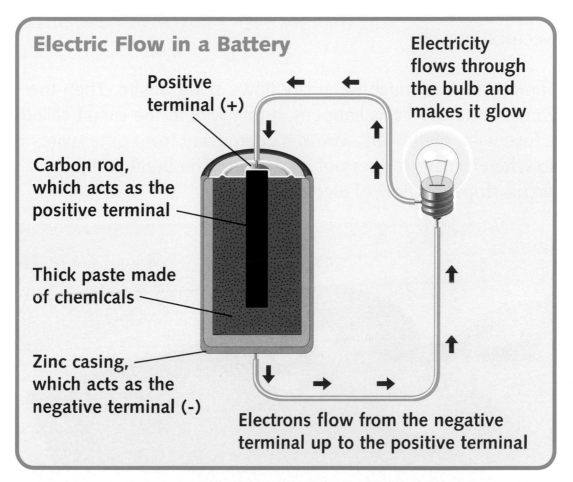

Electric Flow in a Battery

Electricity flows through the bulb and makes it glow

Positive terminal (+)

Carbon rod, which acts as the positive terminal

Thick paste made of chemicals

Zinc casing, which acts as the negative terminal (-)

Electrons flow from the negative terminal up to the positive terminal

▲ A ***chemical reaction*** *produces electrical power from a battery.*

Flat!

Batteries die when their chemicals run out. These can be recharged in some batteries when linked to an electrical circuit. Chemicals inside batteries can burn you. When a battery is dead, give it to an adult. He or she will know how to get rid of it safely.

Home Circuits

Several circuits carry electricity to different areas in your house. An oven uses a lot of electrical power so it uses its own circuit. Another circuit feeds the outlets into which you put plugs. This circuit might also supply the lights with electrical power.

Sometimes, too much electricity flows along a wire. Then the wire overheats. If this happens, a thin wire in the circuit called a fuse wire, melts. This wire is hidden away from other wires so when it melts it does not start a fire. The break in the circuit stops the flow of electricity.

▲A stove will have its own circuit in a home. It uses a lot of electrical power.

MEASURING ELECTRICITY

Volts (V) measure the push of electrical current.
Watts (W) measure the power of electricity.
Amps (A) measure the current.

A fuse box is a metal box found in many homes. Its job is to control the electrical supply coming from the power plant. You don't want too much electricity flowing to an electrical appliance. This can be dangerous.

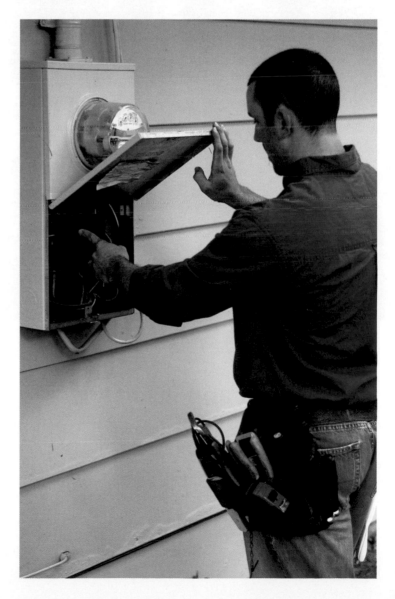

►*Qualified electricians fix problems with electrical circuits or fuse boxes.*

▲*This photograph shows the insulators on a substation.*

Conductors and Insulators

Electricity can flow through a variety of materials. Some are more easy to flow through than others. These are called **conductors**. The electrons move through conductors very easily. Materials such as metals and water are good conductors. Other materials block the flow of electricity. These are called **insulators**. They block the flow because their electrons do not move freely. Plastic and glass are insulators.

Resist!

Electricity flows through materials at different speeds. This is called electrical **resistance**. Controlling the resistance of electric flow controls the volume in a radio. Turning the knob on a radio increases or decreases the length of the copper wire inside. The current has to flow further down a long wire and is weaker. A strong current along a short wire increases the volume.

SPECIAL COATING

Wires are covered in plastic. This keeps the electrical current from jumping out of the metal wires inside.

chapter five

Electricity at Work

Without electricity, our only source of light would be sunlight or candle flames. We would not have hot water or central heating. Electrical energy is useful when turned into heat or light energy.

Look at a lightbulb that is not lit. Inside some you may be able to see a very thin wire. This is called a filament. Electrons have to push hard to get through this thin wire. The heat this creates gives out a glowing light.

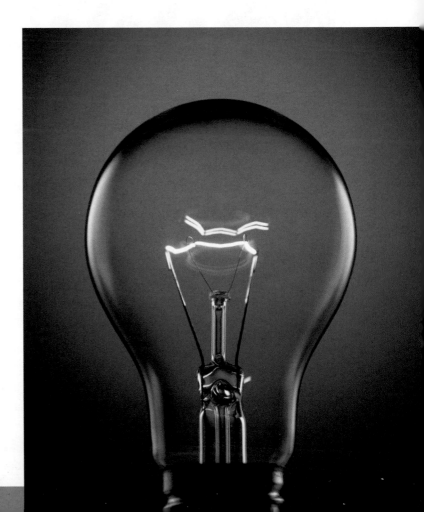

► *This filament is about 6.5 feet (2 meters) long but only one-hundredth of an inch (0.025cm) thick.*

▲In a process called arc welding, electricity produces fierce heat. It can melt metal.

Many people have electric toasters and heaters. These change electrical energy into heat energy. An electrical current flows through wires that create heat energy. The wires or toaster coverings are covered with a material that collects and stores this heat.

A KILOWATT OF POWER

One thousand watts of electricity is a kilowatt. How much power is in a kilowatt? An electric oven will run for twenty minutes. A TV will go for three hours. A 100-watt bulb will have 12 hours. And an electric clock will run for three months.

Keep in Touch

Without electricity, you could not talk on the phone. You could not chat online with a friend. The telephone, the Internet, email, and mobile phones all use electricity. This amazing energy is used in many of today's ways of communication.

◄*From mobile phones to the Internet, modern communication depends upon electricity.*

Moving Pictures!

A television camera turns light and sound into electrical waves. Our televisions turn these waves back into light and sound signals that you can see as your favorite TV program.

Chat

Your voice travels through a microphone in a telephone as sound waves. The waves press against a metal plate that creates an electrical current. This passes into a loudspeaker. The current then turns back into vibrations and sound waves. We hear them as sounds.

Electronics

Electronics is the use of devices to control the movement of electrons creating tiny currents. Devices, such as **microchips**, are built into small circuits. They are used in many machines such as computers, washing machines, and calculators.

◄*Electronic circuit boards may have several tiny microchips.*

On the Move

Electric cars are growing more popular. They do not make as much **pollution** as other fuel-powered vehicles do.

◀Electric cars would reduce pollution with rush-hour traffic.

Under the Hood

An electric car has an electric motor and batteries. You plug the car in when you are not driving. This recharges the batteries. They store the electricity until someone drives the car again. Then the motor takes energy from the batteries. It turns that energy into mechanical energy. This makes the car move.

WITHOUT POWER

One day in 2003, parts of the United States and Canada lost power. This means they had no electricity. It was one of the hottest days of the year. Over 50 million people were without lights. They had no air conditioning. Many businesses could not open. Subways could not run. Everything came to a stop.

▲A tram runs on an electric circuit. Electricity flows from overhead cables, down poles to the driver's controls. The electricity flows through a motor onto the tram track.

chapter six

Electricity and Your World

World temperatures are rising. Glaciers are melting. More extreme weather conditions such as floods and hurricanes are affecting Earth. This is all because of **global warming**. Pollution is one cause of this. Electricity does not create pollution. But some fuels used to produce it do.

▲*Extreme weather conditions, such as hurricanes and tornadoes, seem to be happening more regularly in recent years. Many experts and scientists blame global warming.*

▲*The Toyota Prius is the world's first mass-produced hybrid (meaning 'mixed') car. It can switch between running on gasoline and electricity.*

Saving Energy

We must cut down on the amount of electricity we use. This will help reduce the pollution. Electricity itself does not pollute. But some pollution is caused by burning fuels to make it.

A fuel cell uses the gases hydrogen and oxygen. It turns the energy from these gases into electricity. The only waste or pollution is water! Could these take the place of regular batteries? Regular batteries use up a lot of energy to make.

MAKING A CHANGE

Only 10 percent of the energy used by a regular bulb produces light. The rest is given off as heat. Compact fluorescent lightbulbs (CFLs) use a quarter of the energy that regular lightbulbs use. They last eight times longer. Imagine that every home changed one standard bulb for one compact fluorescent bulb. That would save enough energy to light all the houses in Sacramento, California, for nearly two years!

▲*Fuels such as coal are nonrenewable.*

A Clean Energy?

Some electricity is produced using energy resources that cannot be used up. These include the wind, the Sun, and the movement of waves. This is renewable electricity. This saves our fossil fuels. It also cuts down on pollution.

Coal, natural gas, and oil are called fossil fuels. They formed in Earth over millions of years. However, we are using these fuels very quickly. One day, they will run out. Fuels like these are called nonrenewable.

NUCLEAR POWER

Electricity can be made from nuclear fuel. This is uranium. Electricity made this way causes very little pollution. This material can be very dangerous, however. It can be used to make nuclear weapons. And there is not yet a safe way to dispose of the waste fuel.

From garbage to waves, renewable fuels can generate electricity without creating as much pollution. The heat from the Sun heats mirrors. This heat turns water into steam. The steam powers a generator. That produces electricity.

Biomass is another renewable resource. It also can be used to create electricity. Biomass is the name for materials such as waste wood and garbage. As this material is burned, it creates heat and steam. These turn huge **turbines**, and electricity is created from them.

▼*Using the power from the wind is becoming a more common way to produce electricity.*

Future

To protect the planet, we must use our energy wisely. This includes electricity and the resources with which we make it. At the same time, scientists are discovering new ways to use electricity. Some of these uses are amazing.

Scientists are making devices even smaller, a feature called nanotechnology. Clothes can be fitted with tiny electrical devices to play your favorite tunes. You can download information onto a wafer-thin electronic screen using "electronic ink." Images form as electrically charged tiny black-and-white balls float up and down in liquid.

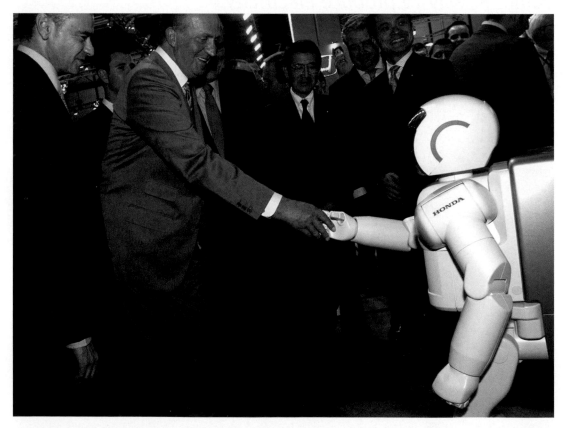

▲*Robots are becoming more and more popular. In Japan, there is a new generation of robots—used for office tasks and housecleaning.*

RESOURCES FOR ALL?

Less than 5 percent of the world's population lives in the United States. But the country uses up one fourth of the world's energy resources. Many people living in the poorer countries of the world do not have easy access to electricity. They walk miles to school. They study by candlelight. Yet these are often the people most affected by extreme weather conditions caused by the effects of pollution.

Glossary

atom (AT uhm) — the smallest pieces of matter

chemical reaction (KEM uh kuhl ree AK shuhn) — when atoms move around and rearrange themselves to make new molecules, or substances

circuit (SUR kit) — a loop along which electricity flows when there are no gaps

conductor (kuhn DUHK tur) — a material through which electricity can flow

electrical current (i LEK tri kuhl KUR uhnt) — a flow of electrical charge

electric motor (i LEK trik MOH tur) — a motor in which electricity is used to create movement

electron (i LEK tron) — a particle inside an atom, made of a negative electrical charge

electronics (i lek TRON iks) — controlling the flow of electrons to create tiny electrical currents

energy (EN ur jee) — the ability to do work

generator (JEN uh ray tur) — a machine that converts mechanical energy into electrical energy

global warming (GLOH buhl WOR ming) — the gradual warming of Earth's climate

grid (grid) — the network of cables and wires which are spread across the country

insulator (IN suh lay tur) — a material through which electricity cannot flow

magnetism (MAG nuh tiz uhm) — an invisible force in some materials that can attract and repel other materials

matter (MAT ur) — the stuff that things are made of, matter is made up of atoms and molecules

microchip (MYE kroh chip) — a very thin piece of silicon with electronic circuits printed on it

neutron (NOO tron) — a particle inside an atom, it has no electrical charge

pollution (puh LOO shuhn) — making land, air, or water dirty

power plant (POU ur plant) — a factory that produces electricity

proton (PROH ton) — a particle inside an atom, made of a positive electrical charge

resistance (ri ZISS tuhnss) — the way a circuit resists the flow of electric current

static electricity (STAT ik i lek TRISS uh tee) — occurs on the surfaces of materials when there is an imbalance of positive and negative charges

transformer (transs FOR mur) — a machine to reduce the power of electrical current

turbine (TUR bine) — an engine driven by water, steam, or gas passing through the blades of a wheel, and making it spin

voltage (VOHL tij) — the measurement of the push of the electrical current

watt (wot) — the measurement of the power of electricity

Further Information

Books
Electricity. Steve Parker and Laura Buller. DK Publishing, 2005.

Electricity and Magnetism. Gerard Cheshire. Smart Apple Media, 2006.

Electricity and the Lightbulb. James Lincoln Collier. Benchmark Books, 2005.

Shocking World of Electricity with Max Axiom, Super Scientist. Liam O' Donnell. Capstone Press, 2005.

Websites to visit
www.eia.doe.gov/kids/energyfacts/sources/electricity.html
Energy Information Administration
This site has a section for kids, which has information on electricity. It also has activity and puzzle pages.

www.southerncompany.com/learningpower/home.asp?mnuOpco=soco&mnuType=lp&mnuItem=oc
Southern Company
This site gives you the history of electricity, and looks at today's power plants.

www.pge.com/microsite/PGE_dgz/body/concepts.html
Pacific Gas and Electric Company
This site shows simply how electricity occurs, along with other electricity facts.

www.sciencemadesimple.com/static.html
Science Made Simple
This site explains static electricity in detail.

www.andythelwelwell.com/blobz/
A guide to electrical circuits.

Index